Floral Mandala Motifs
COLORING BOOK
30 FLOWER-THEMED MANDALAS FOR ADVANCED COLORISTS

KARYN LEWIS

Copyright © 2017 by Karyn Lewis Bonfiglio

FLORAL MANDALA MOTIFS COLORING BOOK:
30 Flower-Themed Mandalas for Advanced Colorists

All rights reserved.

The illustrations in this coloring book are for your personal enjoyment and display. These illustrations may not be reproduced, resold, or used in any commercial manner without express permission by the artist.

ISBN-13: 978-1979179058
ISBN-10: 1979179050

The cover design and all of the illustrations in this coloring book were created by Karyn Lewis Bonfiglio. To see more of her work or to contact her, please visit her website at:

www.karynlewis.com

Printed by CreateSpace.

"If you take a flower in your hand and really look at it, it's your world for a moment."

— *Georgia O'Keeffe*

A Note to the Reader

I love drawing mandalas. For me, the process of creating mandalas is a form of meditation. When starting each new piece I typically sit down at my drawing tablet without a plan and just let the images flow forth. There's no clear path to completion, only the lines and patterns that naturally develop.

For this particular collection of mandalas, I wanted to explore the beauty of flowers. Flowers are so lovely in their own right, and can be drawn in an infinite number of ways—from realistic blossoms to abstract patterns of blooms. I liberally sprinkled each of these mandalas with an abundance of leaves and flowers, while also including the shapes and elements that I personally love most—lines, curves, circles, and order out of chaos.

As you color the mandalas in this book, I hope you too experience the same sense of serenity and joy in your creations that I've felt in mine.

How to Use this Book

Each illustration in this book is single-sided to prevent bleed-through onto the next image. However, it's always good practice to slip a blotter sheet (or two) underneath the page you are coloring to protect the next design.

Try not to dive in and color your mandalas without first using the test page to see how the paper will react to the coloring tool you would like to use.

Above all, when using this book let your creativity flow. Grab your favorite beverage, relax, and most of all, have fun!

Color Test Page

WHAT WILL MY COLORS LOOK LIKE?

Use the boxes above to test out your pens, paints, markers, pastels or pencils, and jot down which brand or type of tool you are using.

Some things to consider: How well does the color spread on the page? Is there bleed-through? How vibrant or soft are the colors? How well does the paper hold up to water-based inks or paints?

Additional pages at the back of this book have been provided for you to practice on. Have fun!

20

Express Yourself
Use this space to doodle, dream, practice, journal or be creative.

Express Yourself
Use this space to doodle, dream, practice, journal or be creative.

Express Yourself
Use this space to doodle, dream, practice, journal or be creative.

Express Yourself
Use this space to doodle, dream, practice, journal or be creative.

About the Author

Karyn Lewis is an illustrator, writer, knitter, crafter, mom, and wife. She received a Bachelor of Fine Arts degree in drawing from Colorado State University, and worked in the newspaper industry for a number of years before focusing her attention on her freelance career. She currently lives in South Bend, Indiana, with her husband, Jeremy, and their son, William, as well as a dog, a cat, and two, rescued rats.

Please visit her author page on Amazon.com to browse the other coloring books she has available at: www.amazon.com/author/karynlewis

To see more of her illustration work, please visit her website at: www.karynlewis.com

SHE CAN ALSO BE FOUND ONLINE AT:

Facebook: www.facebook.com/karynlewisillustration

Twitter: www.twitter.com/nyrak

Instagram: www.instagram.com/yadykaryn

YouTube: www.youtube.com/user/yadykaryn